D0618495

The
First
Best
Thing

Written and illustrated by
Erin K. Rothman

ISBN 978-0-615-79566-9

First Edition

Written and illustrated by Erin K. Rothman
Layout and photography by Vincent Bachmann

Dedicated to anyone who has ever been able to fit into a garbage can (albeit proven involuntarily), too ugly to look into a mirror, too embarassed to stand up for themselves, or too lonely to try.

I never thought knees actually knocked. I read about it in books, but I never heard of such a thing happening in real life. Which is why it was quite a shock to look down and see my knees knocking, one against the other. I looked up to see a classroom full of mean, bored, and contemptful eyes. Not a nice face in the group. I introduced myself (Hi, I'm Erin. I just moved here from Illinois.) to silence and managed to get my ridiculously wobbly legs back to my desk.

Somehow my body knew what my conscience would (could?) not comprehend. I was surrounded by hate, and frankly, at age 11, that's not the easiest thing to add to a list of adolescent issues.

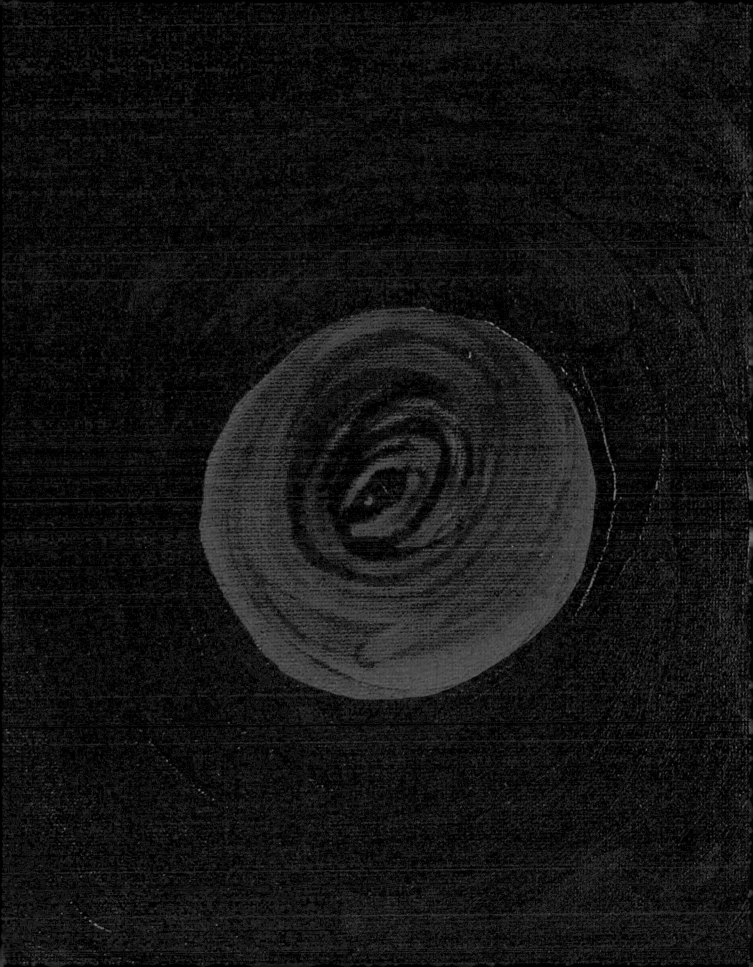

I could go into great detail regarding the all-consuming anguish. Maybe just a little bit.

Every morning I would walk really, really quickly to and from school so no one could talk to me, if they even wanted to. The shame was too much.

I hated my sisters for being so pretty and so happy. (*"Are these your daughters? These two are just beautiful!"* ... "There were three of us.)

I avoided mirrors because I was horrified by my face and reminded why no one would be my friend.

I locked myself in my bedroom every day and every night, listening to how happy my family was without me, knowing that they would always be happier without me.

M

y 6th grade teacher told me I dressed like a slut. (That woman must have had a freaky, dirty mind. I was 11 for god's sake!)

If my mom wouldn't take me to the store with her, I thought it was because she was embarrassed to be seen with her ugliest daughter.

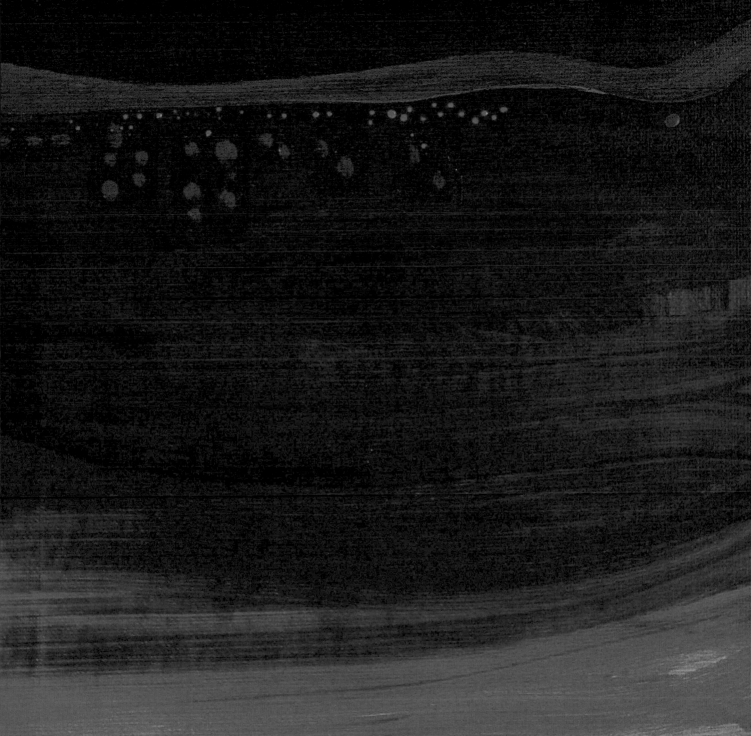

Whenever I had to wear dress shoes for school, I would walk flat-footed to avoid the clickety-clack of fancy shoes on a hard floor, and so avoided attention.

A little kid walked up to me in school one day and said "Wow! You are really ugly." He shook his head and walked off. He couldn't hear me respond in a tiny voice, "I know."

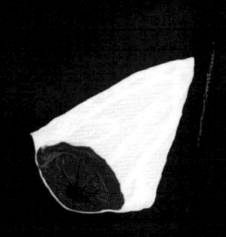

I n 7th grade, Tim the bully hit me so hard on the back of my head with his textbook that he gave me a concussion.

I n 8th grade, the girl gangs of middle school liked to stuff me in garbage cans, usually because I didn't have something they wanted. Or anyone to tell them to stop.

Despite all of that...attention... I was convinced (I hoped?) that I didn't exist. Statistically speaking, it was impossible. So I wasn't there. And nothing was really happening to me or anyone else. I stayed really, really still for hours, proving that no one could see or hear me.

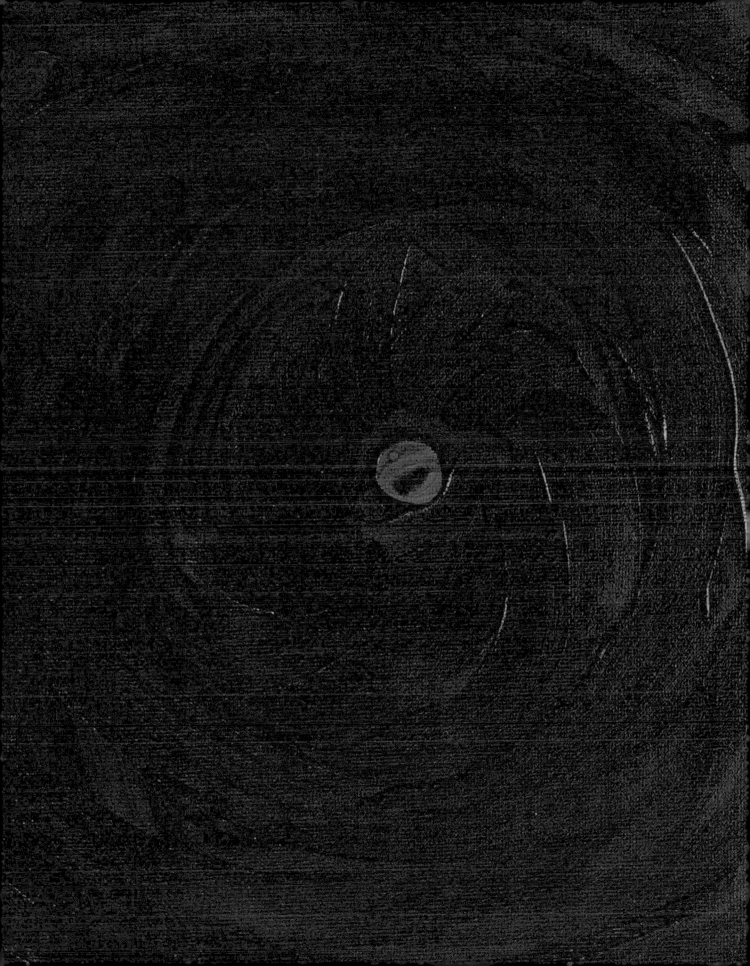

Maybe it doesn't sound like a lot, not really, but add that to moving to a new town, having no friends, wearing big plastic-framed glasses, hiding my braces, and sticking back my well-damaged hair (a result of an ill-timed perm when I was 10). It was devastating to be hated so much.

I was filled with so much hate and disgust and terror every moment of every day that I would have been willing to do anything to stop it. But I didn't. It took me over and I drowned in it.

Somehow, two years went by.

I crept out of my room to see my family. Dad said something funny and I laughed. That laughter was so shocking that I stopped immediately. And then, slowly, let out a bit more. I felt my eyes light up, just a bit. It was THE CRAZIEST MOMENT OF MY LIFE. A flash of joy! How I missed it! And I didn't even notice when it disappeared so long ago.

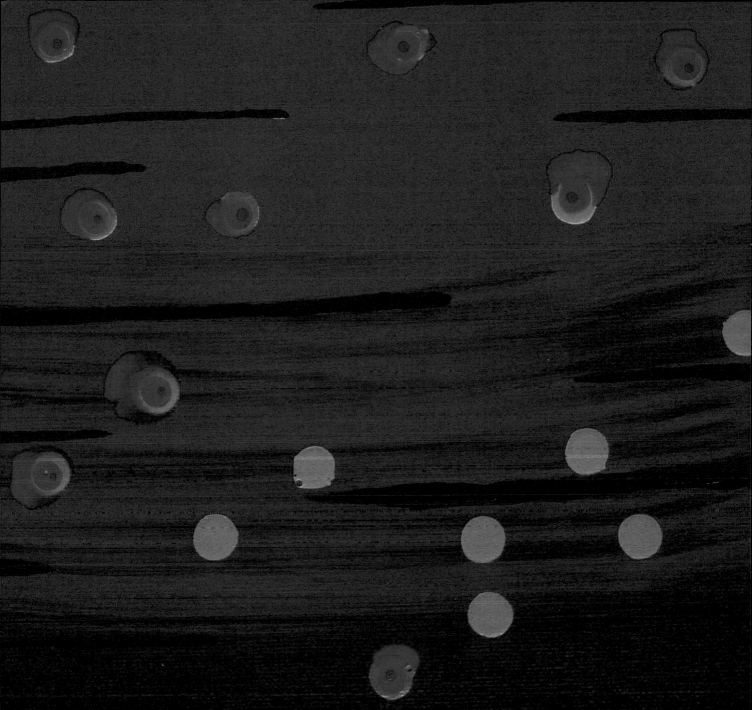

A few weeks later I was riding the bus to school. It was winter and it was snowing. Big, beautiful, fluffy, Christmas-carols-and-snowglobe flakes falling from the sky. I scrunched myself deeper into the seat at the front of the bus. I thought about how much I hated snow.

And then, oddly, I stopped myself. And I thought—and this gets weird—I love snow. And my heart fluttered a little. I sat up straighter and repeated it to myself. I love snow! I love snow! And I love the trees in the snow and how the ice and the flakes sparkle in the headlights.

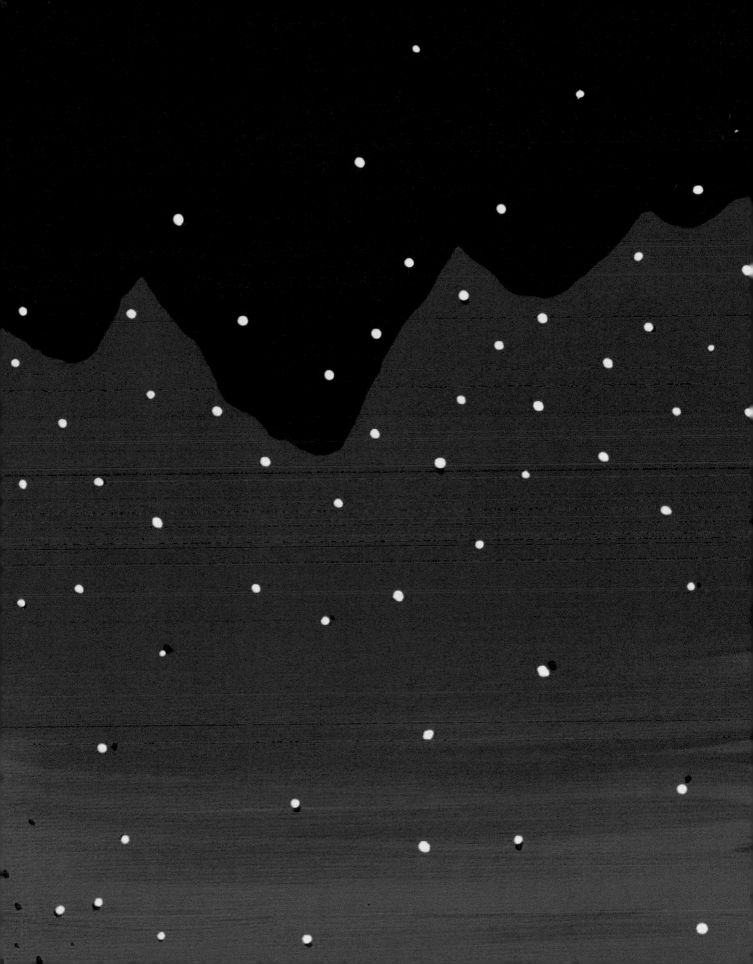

And I decided then that I would never think a thought of hate again.

Easier said than done.

Angry thoughts get easily embedded, especially when they have built up over several years and have adolescence, puberty, and a great deal of emotional instability to grow and nurture them.

They were everywhere. They overwhelmed me, and prior to the snowflake episode, I hadn't even noticed that they existed. That they were a part of me.

Making them disappear took
some practice. Every single
thought I had invoked at
least some twinge of anger, disgust,
hatred, or pain.

So I reversed it.

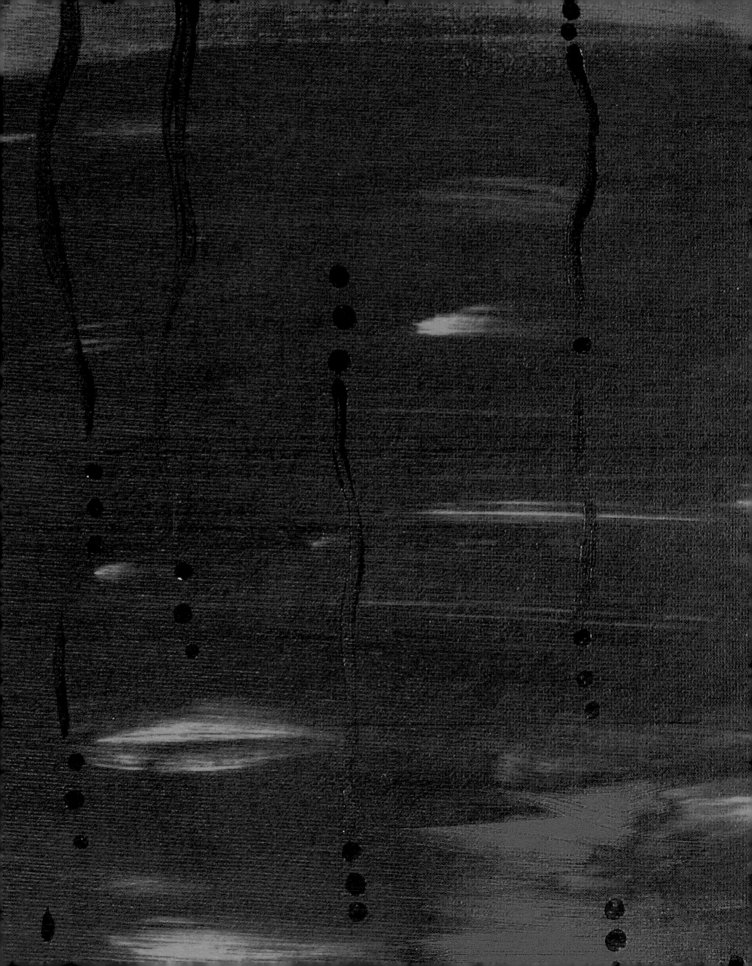

I hate the heat. I hate the sun. I hate the sky and being awake. *(No, I actually really love to be warm.)*

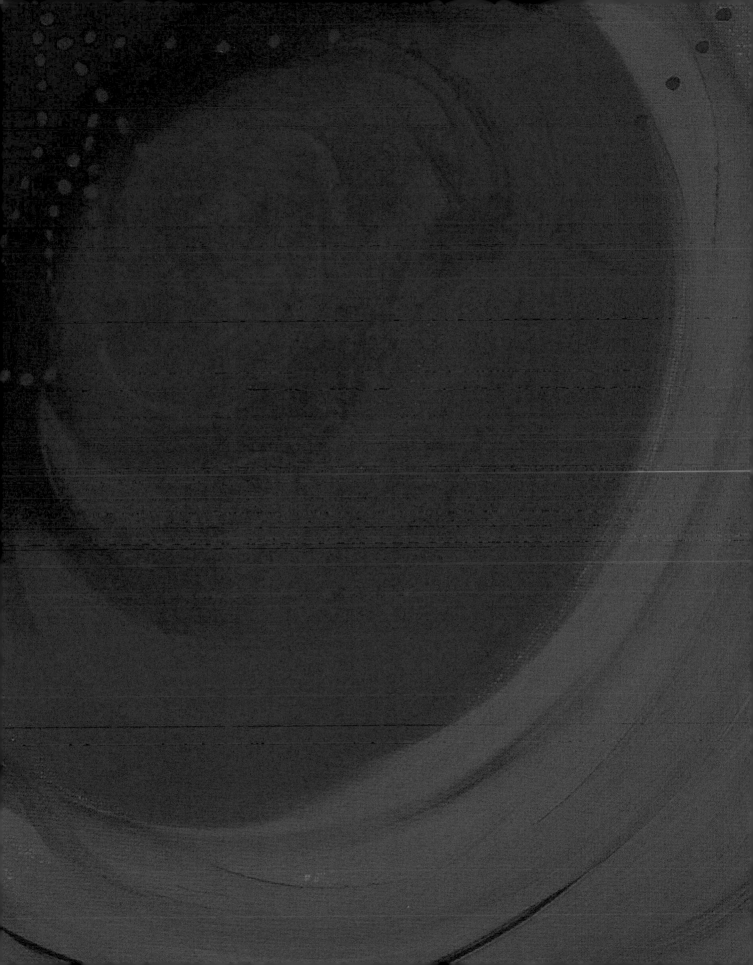

I hate sunsets. They're overrated and nothing special and kind of make me sick. *(They're actually quite lovely.)*

I hate riding in the car, going anywhere with anyone. *(Although, when I think about it, it's rather enjoyable.)*

My god, I am so ugly! So ugly. I hate my face. *(I have beautiful eyes....)*

A
nd so on, all day, every day,
for years.

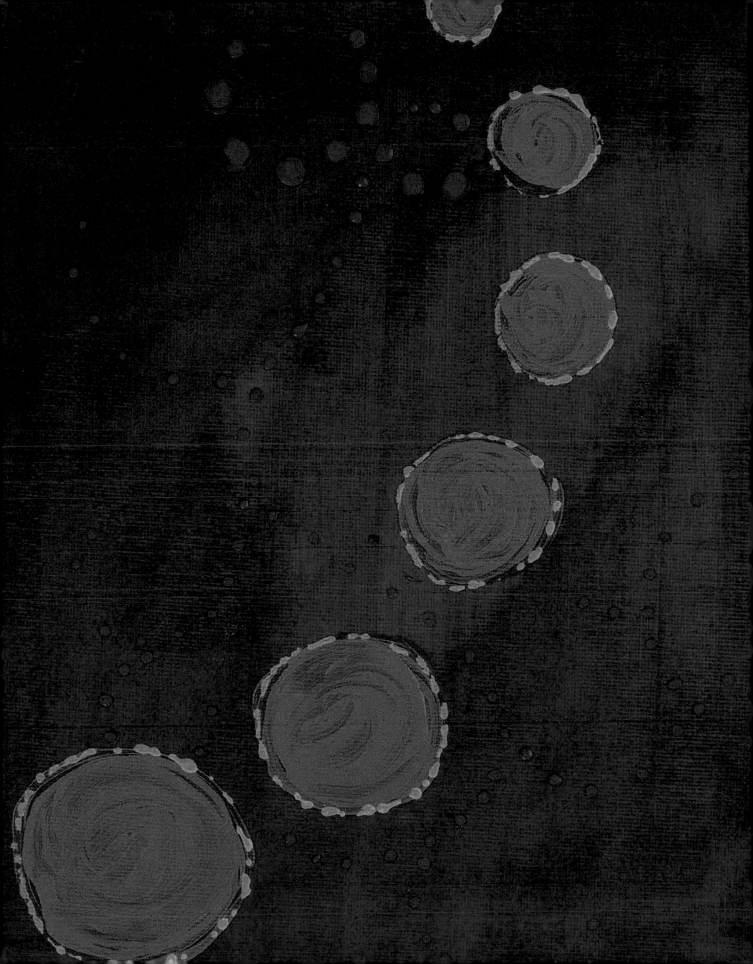

Until they stopped.

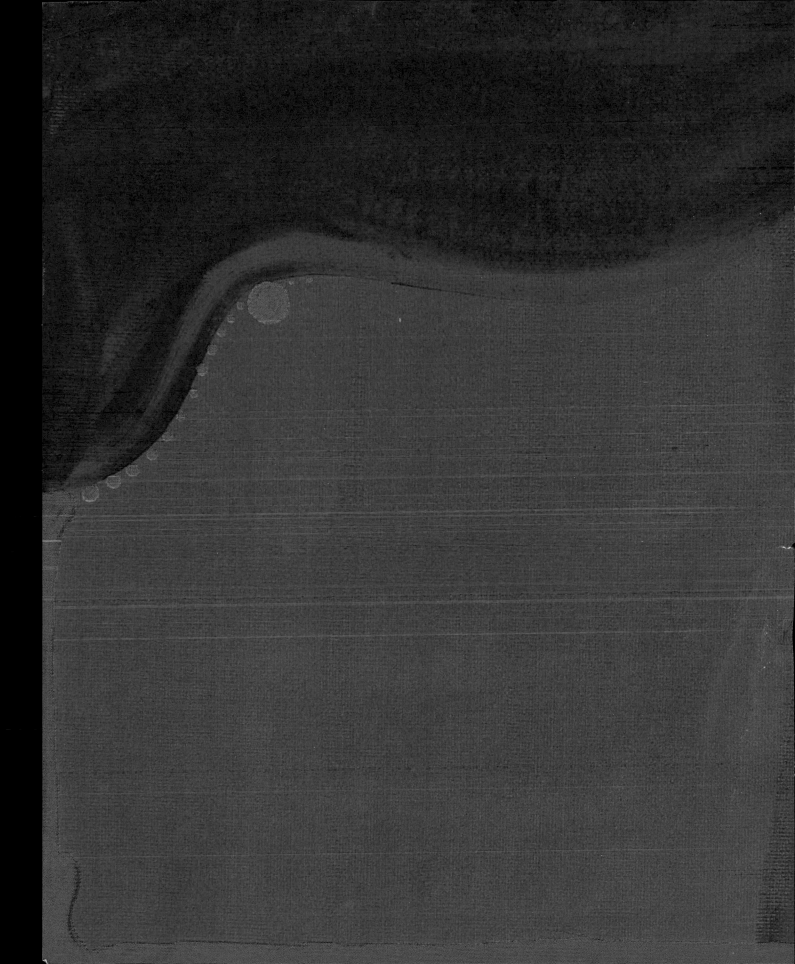

Of course, they don't completely stop forever. I still have to force them toward the positive.

It's the first best thing I
ever did for myself.

CPSIA information can be obtained
at www.ICGtesting.com
Printed in the USA
LVIC06n1506181013
357590LV00035B/227